How to Transform

Yourself

in the

One Billion

Dollars Lady

GIULIANA MISIR

Paperback: 978-1-967820-98-6
eBook: 978-1-967820-99-3
Library of Congress Control Number: 2025912900

This is a work of nonfiction.

Ordering Information:

Prime Seven Media
518 Landmann St.
Tomah City, WI 54660

Printed in the United States of America

Table of Contents

"A QUICK GUIDE TO BECOME A BILLION DOLLAR WOMAN"

Leave your old self behind and upgrade to the sky

M y name is Giuliana Misir, I am 50 years old, and I decided to write this little book to help all the women in the world who, like me, have had to face all kinds of difficulties.

I am not a doctor, I am not a psychologist, I am not even a trainer, even if I could be, I am just a woman who has lived 50 years of love and lack of love, betrayals and strong bonds, happiness and desperation, wealthy and poverty, I have lost everything and regained everything, love, health, money, but above all, serenity.

I have been through all kinds of difficulties in my life. I have fallen from above and I have gotten up again. I have learned to react even when life has really knocked me down.

You, my friend who is reading this, will say: 'But like all of us, you too will have had difficulties...'

I hope not, exactly like everyone else, otherwise, the female world would be a disaster. If you all have, at some point, problems in your life, I have had them all:

Since birth, I was not accepted by my own mother

I lived a terrible marriage with a billionaire in beautiful Italy, but he, the husband, turned out to be a terribly selfish, narcissistic, often sadistic, and ruthless man.

My best friend, loved like a sister since childhood, who has an affair with my husband (in what atrocious way was my heart broken?...)

"A QUICK GUIDE TO BECOME A BILLION DOLLAR WOMAN"

A quick divorce from which I came out without a penny, without a home, without a job

The dramatic loss of two pregnancies

Depression and anorexia (it goes without saying)

An advanced stage of cancer from which I managed to recover, and then:

Rebuild a job, a home, a life

Rebuild my physical and mental well-being.

Forgive and love my mother and my ex-husband

Economically returning to live at a higher level in every sense.

What can I say more? My life has been a merry-go-round of good and bad situations, I learned to manage and to organise my inner self in order to limitate damage and maximise all good things, first of all, my personal potential.

Finding love again with a balanced and loving partner.

Today, finally, I'm living a happy life.

Chapter 1

A like AMORE (LOVE) ..LOVE...

I was born into a young family; my parents were in their early twenties, and my grandparents in their early forties.

They say that a child chooses the family he or she arrives in. If that's the case, I chose them because they were young and loved each other. That's what I like to believe.

I remember my parents as a beautiful couple in love. Surely when I was born, they weren't ready to be parents, so they 'passed' me on to my grandparents. My grandparents welcomed me with love, they did everything they could for my development, but there was no continuity in my life, I was a 'package' that went alternately from my grandparents' country house to my parents' apartment in the city, from Sundays at mass in the countryside to weekends parties in the city.

And here the problems begin....... My young mother went in competition with my young grandmother, her mother-in-law, both in sharing the love for her husband, my dad and in sharing the affection that I, at the time a child, showed to both of them, but perhaps a little more to my grandmother, because she represented more of the maternal archetype than my young mother who smoked cigarettes, danced disco and devoted herself to her career. Furthermore, I grew up with the inconvenience of having been born when she was too young, not yet ready, I represented an impediment to her evolution, her career, and her freedom.

In the years that followed my mother always proved to be not yet ready to love and accept me, everything I did was never enough, I was not beautiful, I was not smart, I was not as cool as her friends' daughters, my mistakes were always catastrophic to her and my small victories were nothing important.

And here comes the first trauma: the pain of not being loved by your mother, of not being appreciated by your mother, of never being encouraged by your mother. Rejection.

So I grew up with the constant feeling of not being worth anything, of not being anyone, of not deserving much. This trauma lasts throughout life and never heals.

Chapter 1

A like AMORE (LOVE)
..LOVE...

Do you recognize yourself in this situation? The trauma of not being accepted, of not being loved, of not being worthy enough. The origin of this trauma can be the behavior of the mother, of the father or of any person in our life who plays that type of role.

I repeat, I am not a psychologist, but I can share with you that this trauma is highly disabling, you carry it with you for your entire life and it will affect you in everything you do and in all your important choices.

So I spent a good part of my life not giving value to myself, being amazed every time I got a prize (What, to me?....), every time I got the job I wanted it seemed like I had gotten that position by lucky chance and certainly not for any merit of my own, every time I liked a man I thought: 'But imagine if he will fall in love with me...', and so on.......

I spent many years not believing in myself.

I was young and beautiful, to make ends meet, I also worked as a model, but deep down I thought I was ugly, certainly less beautiful than the others, and if they chose me, it was certainly pure luck.

Raise your hand if you recognize yourself in this type of situation! You have all my sympathy, my friend, if I could I would give you a hug and tell you that all this feeling is not true, this low perception of yourself was created by someone often involuntarily, but this is your mental cage that will not allow you to live fully and develop your entire personality as you would like. You would like it, but you do not have the courage.

They say that to want to escape from a prison, you must first understand that you are imprisoned. Here, those who have the trauma of rejection believe that they are not worth enough, that they are not beautiful enough, good enough, successful enough, capable enough, strong enough, etc., this is the prison you must escape from.

Get out of 'I am not enough'.

How do you do it?

A like AMORE (LOVE)
..LOVE...

It is not easy. You have to love yourself.

When I say this, I don't mean doing stupid shopping to gratify yourself, I don't mean masturbating (we'll talk about that later), nor even hunting for 'admirers', no, I mean that you have to love, respect, and trust yourself. It's hard work.

Try now, in this moment, to make a list of all the things that you think you've done well and compliment yourself, rejoice with yourself, remind yourself how good you were at doing them well and give yourself a hug, try to remember the feeling you had when your program came true and try to maintain that feeling of joy and satisfaction while looking at yourself in the mirror. Good job!

You will have to do this exercise more often, even every day, if you can.

Every time you set a goal in life or work, prepare yourself well, because nothing is achieved without the right preparation, and go in front of the mirror and tell yourself that you are fully, I repeat, fully capable of doing what you want and you will get what you have prepared to do because you deserve it. You are worthy. You deserve the big prize!

When you have learned to love yourself and trust yourself, you will be a better partner and a better mother, a friend, an aunt, a much better person in the lives of others.

Love yourself and do not judge yourself, do not punish yourself for your mistakes, do not torture yourself psychologically, and do not allow anyone to do it.

Every time you succeed in something, be happy and remember that you deserved it.

If you do not succeed in something and you care deeply about it, keep trying. Without feeling guilty and punishing yourself. Just try again.

A for AMORE
LOVE again

S elf-love as a way of life.

You're a woman. The most beautiful creature in the world.

All human creatures can create, generate, but you, my dear, can also generate a new human being. WOW! How big is this?

But to be fully a woman, to be evolved 360 degrees, you need....LOVE.

Yes, we always come back to the word love because it is the key to the life of all living beings, of all creation, and we women must be healthy carriers of love. That is, to have a lot of love for ourselves, this then translates into self-esteem, a good self-image, feeling good about ourselves, and many other positive things. To be able to give love to those who live with us, we must first love ourselves. Did you already know that? Yes, but here I will tell you more.

Here is a list of things to do to give yourself more love, to become a more beautiful woman inside and out:

1. Cry when you feel the need.

2. Laugh when you feel the need.

3. Rest. Sleep. Sleep is a cure for the body, soul, and mind.

4. Never go on a diet.

I know this goes against entire libraries of teachings on how to live a healthy life, but I will tell you that once you reach a good level of consciousness, your mind will shape your body. (I must point out that this excludes people who, for serious medical reasons, must follow a diet)

Chapter 2

A for AMORE
LOVE again

I will try to explain this principle better:

We, human beings, are born on planet Earth that offers us an infinite variety of foods. Of course, here I am referring only to natural, unprocessed foods, cooked in the simplest way possible. Only this is the true concept of food and nutrition.

So, if you learn to eat natural food, if you learn to drink lots of good water and natural drinks, you can indulge in a glass of wine every now and then or maybe some champagne. We have already established the guidelines for the best diet to follow. For the rest, eat everything you like, how and when you want. The secret? Don't overdo it. Watch the quantities.

As you follow this rule, over time, your body will understand that it is regularly fed with good, natural foods, hydrated with water and herbal teas, and will ask to eat a little less. You will be amazed to realize that after a while of following this eating pattern, your body will stabilize its weight, you will lose the excess weight on your own, and remain stable over time.

You just have to be faithful to this simple principle of nutrition: natural, unprocessed food, water, and everything will be ok. Always try to eat not too much, then your body will regulate itself.

Luckily, I learned this simple thing from an old monk in an Orthodox monastery when I was about 22 years old. I put it into practice and since then (I'm 50 today), my body weight has always been the same, between 53 and 54 kg. I have never eaten junk food for almost 30 years, and I don't even want to. The first few times it was hard for me to give up the burger, the colorful and sweet drink, the donuts, but I got used to cooking my own food, including desserts, today, thank God, there are so many places that serve healthy food, so I don't miss anything, but my plate is never big and my meals are two in a day, that's enough for me.

(Of course, those who do sports should have a different diet, but we are talking about how a normal and healthy person should eat.)

Also, know that industrially produced and processed foods are studied and contain substances that are addictive, so you will want more and more, but a good plate of natural food will fill you up for 5-6 hours without making you gain weight.

A for AMORE
LOVE again

One more thing about food: food is a form of love that planet Earth gives us. Good food is healthy. Good health means fertility for us women and a long life.

5. Learn to fast. Fasting is also part of a healthy lifestyle. Fasting cleanses your entire body from the inside. If you have never done it, start by skipping a meal, without eating more at the next one. I usually fast one day a week, I don't eat anything for 24 hours, and I drink lots of water, take hot baths, read, and rest. I usually do this on a day that I don't have to work. Try it too.

Fasting was already practiced thousands of years ago as part of a cure, but also as part of a spiritual path.

If you learn to fast, you will slowly improve both your physical and mental health.

I learned to appreciate fasting when, years ago, I had to deal with cancer. So I went to a retreat where they made me fast for a week. (And not only that).

6. (I should have put it in point 1) BREATHE!

Learn to breathe deeply, with full lungs.

Open the windows of your house every morning and take deep breaths. Breathe in through your mouth, down your throat, into your lungs, and down into your belly. Do this several times. Even while you work, stop for 2 minutes to take deep breaths. Your body and brain need oxygen.

You know, life begins and ends with a deep breath.

BREATHE!

7. Learn to be alone. Solitude is precious. If you know how to be alone, you will be a good companion for your partner.

Chapter 2

A for AMORE
LOVE again

Let me explain: knowing how to be alone means having more time for yourself, to get to know yourself, to follow your passions, your own pace.

If you happen to not have a partner at this time, know that you have a great opportunity to be with yourself and to dedicate yourself to yourself, to improve your person and personality, before finding a new partner with whom you will have to settle.

Even if you live as a couple, it is important that each of you make time to pursue your hobbies and spend some time on your own.

8. Travel alone. Not all the time, but every once in a while, go to a beautiful place that means something to you and enjoy the ride. Of course, make sure you travel safely, but for God's sake, get out of your cozy nest and experience something new! You'll learn more about the world, and you'll learn more about yourself.

9. Move. Get moving, walk, run, swim, go for a walk, jump rope, and do physical exercises.

10. (and now comes the best part) You have to make love. Making love (I didn't say sex) is a process that gives so many advantages from a physical, psychological, emotional, and chemical point of view.

When masculine energy unites with feminine energy (especially in a relationship of true love), the health and personality of both partners benefit infinitely.

11. Masturbate. Yes, I said it.

Masturbation is part of your sexual life. It doesn't matter if you have a partner or not.

If you are in a relationship, it may happen that your partner is unable to bring you to orgasm. Masturbation can be an additional fun to share with him.

If you are alone, you do well to masturbate every now and then.

Having an orgasm regularly is necessary for physical and mental health.

Chapter 2

A for AMORE
LOVE again

Warning! Masturbation is addictive, so....handle with care! 😁

12. Well, now we move from the profane to the sacred: you must dedicate time to your spiritual exercises, which can be praying, meditating, writing a journal, reading......

A woman who loves herself must take care of her body, but also of her spirit.

Reading is always a good practice, I mean reading good books that help you evolve. Today, there are also audiobooks and many educational conferences and podcasts online, but nothing evolves and gives the refinement of the spirit like good literature......

13. Try to raise your cultural level. How? By reading quality books, going to see shows, exhibitions, and museums.

If you can, travel to broaden your culture, visit the Louvre (and Paris), Florence and the Uffizi, Rome, Marrakech, the castles in Transylvania, etc, etc...... The whole world is full of places that can teach us art, history and culture let's go and discover them! (My brand new guide on the 100 most beautiful places in the world that you absolutely must see is coming soon!)

14. This is a cool one: cancel all your subscriptions to Pay per view, cheap movies, tv entertainment, stand up channels and all that shit.

I read an article that says that in America, the average user is present approximately 58 hours a week on one of these platforms. What??? 58 hours watching TV series??? ...in most cases, very low quality productions that do nothing but steal your time! ..And I'll tell you more: prolonged use of low-quality media material lowers your IQ, in short, it makes you more stupid.

So, to evolve your personality, stop getting intoxicated by social media and cheap tv. Start reading a new book a week or, at least, a book a month. I would start with the classics.

If you want to become the billion-dollar woman, the refined lady that every woman would want as a friend and every man would want as a partner, you have to be cultured.

A for AMORE
LOVE again

A good book is a good cure for the soul and a new upgrade for your brain.

15. Drugs, alcohol, and rock and roll........

An elegant and refined woman will never use drugs of any kind.

Once you have detoxified your body and are back in your best physical and psychological shape, why alter your perceptions by using drugs?

Your brain will be able to give you the right answer in every situation, your body will always give you the right sensations, and you will not need substances of any kind to relax or have fun.

When you are in balance, your body produces the chemistry needed to feel satisfied after a good meal, happy after a healthy sexual relationship, relaxed after a bit of movement, genuine joy every time you achieve a result you cared about, a feeling of peace and stability every time you read a good book, or meditate, or relax while looking at the sea or a nice fire in the fireplace.

Your healthy, balanced body is capable of producing a whole host of chemicals to protect your health and well-being at exactly the right time and for the right purpose, far better than any chemical industry in the world.

16. The Hugs

Remember to always hug your loved ones, hug yourself, and cuddle your pets. Every day, at least one hug.

When you have learned to hug yourself, then your loved ones, then your pets, then your friends...then you will be able to hug the world and receive its hug.

Remember? I said it from the beginning; in the end, everything is LOVE.

17. Every day, you say I LOVE YOU to someone. If you don't have anyone to say it to yet, start with yourself. In any case, always start with yourself.

EVOLUTION HURTS

Y our life is a journey. Everybody tells you that. It's true.

Life is evolution. Life is an infinite lesson to learn. It works like that: you live, you have your own experiences to pass through.

Like a tree that goes through the seasons and even in the same season has good days and bad days, too much scorching sun, too much rain, wind, insects, and animals that threaten it.... but the tree has only one thing to do: die or become taller, more beautiful, stronger.

You are this tree that goes through the seasons of life, you have to enjoy the good seasons when they are there and prepare to face the bad seasons that will make you suffer, but will make you stronger and when you are truly strong and spring comes, you will be able to blossom like a beautiful tree that has overcome the winter, has transformed the snow and ice into pure sap that flows in its veins and is now blossoming, spreading perfume around and if, attracting bees, beautiful butterflies, birds that want to live there and it becomes the beautiful plant that attracts everyone's attention and love.

Life is made up of experiences, periods...shall we call them seasons? that you will have to overcome anyway.

Decide if these seasons will knock you down, turn you into a little creeping plant on the ground, or if you want to grow into that flowering tree that everyone will love.

The amazing girl everyone wants, the billion-dollar woman you want to be, is right inside you; you just have to manifest it.

Your transformation continues..

When you, my dear, yes, you, are already well along the journey with and towards your true self, you will realize that your life will begin to change.

EVOLUTION HURTS

Know that when you have reached a significant point in your evolution, you will suddenly become unrecognizable to many old friends, some will leave you, no longer understanding you, because they were in relationship with the old you. Do not be bitter, not all friendships are made to last.

More new bonds will be formed.

But there is one thing: an evolved person knows how to be happy alone (remember?) and will not accept into his circle people who do not share his values.

I remember my period of loneliness between the separation from my first husband and the beginning of the relationship with my current partner.

At first it took me time to come to terms with the breakup, then time to forgive, time to accept that it was all over and to adjust to the new situation.

But I still remember that during that time of 'solitude' I didn't feel lonely for a moment. I was free! I had myself and I started from myself.

First, I rested and began to accept myself as I am. I remember the first time, going shopping alone in Milan, a gentleman approached me in a shop and complimented me, we talked and he invited me to dinner. It wasn't time for me to date yet, but I finally felt the joy and satisfaction of feeling admired and desired again after years of reproaches, arguments, bad things and indifference.

I spent about two years alone, initially focusing only on my work, then I dedicated myself completely to myself: I organized my new apartment, I took all the time I had to rest, to do yoga. I often went to the seaside completely alone, without it weighing on me for even a moment. I must say that I was also very lucky to have my beloved dog Jeep who today rests in the garden of my house under a pomegranate tree. He was a loving companion who always followed me and it is also thanks to him that I was able to recover well from depression, tears, and feelings of guilt.

EVOLUTION HURTS

Lesson #1: Learn to forgive those who have hurt you (God, it's hard!)

Lesson #2: Learn to forgive yourself for everything that happened.

In some cases, you could have done better, you could have made different choices, but....that's how it went. Stop beating yourself up and look forward.

Lesson no. 3: In your heart forgive, hug your ex-partner who made you suffer, say goodbye, thank him and let him go, let him go. Really. To move on you must not still be attached to the person you previously loved. Leave him for real, stop thinking about him, his life, what he has done, does or will do. Inside you, you really have to leave him free. Leave him, so you too will be free.

Lesson No. 4: Don't Repeat the Same Mistakes, Otherwise You'll Have the Same Problems

Lesson #5 Invest in yourself

The first thing is to regain your positive energy. (If necessary, review the rules we saw at the beginning).

Everything will start again from the new you, from your new energy.

What an evolved woman looks like

The woman you want to become, the billion-dollar woman, is always in the best shape possible.

First of all, she is confident, and it shows. An evolved woman radiates a certain positive energy; she walks with her head held high, confident, smiles, and treats others with kindness. She never loses control, because those who do not control themselves do not control others.

An evolved woman always has a good physical appearance. It is not necessarily about being a great beauty on the cover but, if she is an evolved person, she keeps her weight under control, does not eat junk food, does not use drugs, takes care of her body and does physical exercises, so she can only be a woman in the best version of her physical shape and, remember, beyond physical shape, attitude is what makes the difference.

The elegance that an evolved woman must exhibit is not necessarily an elegance studied and obtained by buying lots of fashionable clothes, but rather, it is the elegance of being.

When she enters a room, all eyes will see her. She never raises her voice but makes herself heard, and she is never vulgar but attracts attention.

How does the billion-dollar woman dress?

An evolved woman will always dress in the most appropriate manner according to the place, the people she meets, and the situation.

It is not necessary to spend a lot of money on clothes and accessories, but invest a small budget in quality trousers that enhance your silhouette, skirts that are appropriate for your age and body type, never short after 30 and if your legs are not perfect; a few white shirts always save the day, in winter a nice quality sweater that follows the line of your body (at Christmas, for goodness sake, abandon those horrible sweaters with reindeer, I would outlaw them with a presidential decree!). Over anything, even over jeans, a nice jacket gives a great contour to the body. Avoid furs and puffy duvets, instead invest in a nice coat with a slim line, elegant and timeless. Shoes must be comfortable but not too much during the day and absolutely elegant in the evening, no matter how much pain they may cause.

What an evolved woman looks like

HOW TO TRANSFORM YOURSELF IN THE ONE BILLION DOLLARS LADY

Underwear should always be sexy. No excuses.

I sleep naked, because no garment can be sexier than my skin in intimacy. Any lace blouses or similar must be removed before getting under the sheets.

The Billion Dollar Woman Is Elegant Even Naked

The Jewels

NEVER wear fake, gross, or vulgar jewelry.

An evolved woman can and should only wear real jewels and precious stones. Only gold or platinum, only authentic stones.

In the past, precious gold jewels with precious stones were given to queens and noblewomen, for slaves and servants only accessories in iron, wood, leather, fabric or other. You are now a queen, no concessions to bad taste.

Tattoos

Remember, your beautiful and clean body does not need to be marked with ink, pierced with piercings. Your beautiful ears just need to wear a nice pair of precious earrings. And that's it.

This, my friend, is the lesson I myself have had to learn the hard way.

Seeing yourself as not beautiful and believing that by surgically improving yourself you can improve your life, that is, intervening from the outside by the hand of a stranger (who hopefully will do a good job) and not intervening from the inside by evolving your personality..........It's a question of luck.....

What an evolved woman looks like

However, if for various reasons that should never be judged, you have decided to resort to cosmetic surgery, evaluate everything carefully and, remember, less is more.

Sure, today we have many tools to correct small imperfections, maintain beautiful skin and technology that helps us age better and more slowly, but we must not abuse them.

Of course, you should avoid puffy lips, long false eyelashes, exaggeratedly puffy cheekbones and breasts that would explode in any situation, as well as a swollen bottom that deforms you.

Manners

Beyond your physical appearance, how you dress and what jewelry you wear, your attitude, your manners, your behavior will say everything about you and are the basis for creating new relationships. BEWARE!

From the stars to the stables

How to be happy, unhappy, anorexic, and totally poor.

Many years ago, when I was younger and a beautiful woman, I met a man who bewitched me.

I was already very much courted, invitations to go out to dinners, cocktails, parties, I had no shortage, but when I met him, a brilliant businessman, eternal Italian elegance, excellent manners, luxury cars, he traveled for business and to meet me (we lived in different countries) making appointments in ultra-luxury hotels and the best restaurants in the world, I laid my soul at his feet.

He was rich and that helped a lot, but it was his personality, his wonderful charm and the great self-confidence that he managed to transmit to me too, that won me over. Compared to him, all the men in the world seemed small, insufficient, stupid. I was madly in love with him. It was a magic that lasted about 10 years.
Our relationship was perfect for a while, he was sincerely in love and, even though we worked a lot, we carved out wonderful weekends in Monte Carlo, days in Capri, boat holidays in the Greek islands or little escapades on the top floor of some luxury hotel in Dubai.

We got married without a ceremony, in the presence of a few family members and friends and...not long after, slowly, slowly, the magic began to dissipate.

Not long after I discovered that my wonderful husband was cheating on me, even in a banal way with some of his employees, not necessarily prettier than me. The arguments and fights began. We went out to social parties in elegant clothes and with smiles on our faces, but when we got home we no longer spoke to each other, we slept in separate rooms and I got sick.I got sick of love. I suffered because I missed his love, I missed his body in my bed, every word he said had become wickedness that hurt me, he behaved as if he didn't want me anymore, I still loved him, my heart was torn by the lack of love and by his, now, indifference. From the angel he was at the beginning he had become a demon that hurt me in a thousand ways making me die inside.

From the stars to the stables

I suffered like hell, while from the outside, friends and family continued to see the fairytale image.

One day I decided to talk to my mother about it and she said to me: "Do you realize that millions of women in the world would like to be in your place? All men cheat, you'll get used to it. ...What is this story that you're suffering?! Are you unhappy?!! Look at yourself: you travel in luxury cars, you spend on a dinner what I earn in a month and you're full of jewels. You have a good husband who offers you all this, before him you were nobody. If he cheats on you he's not the only one who does it, but you have to live with it. He doesn't respect you? What does that mean? Who do you think you are? You don't realize how lucky you are."

I thought he was probably right and continued like this for a while longer, but the situation did not improve. My husband became completely absent both physically and emotionally and I was in pieces.

One day, poor me, I decided to cheat on him. I decided to meet up with another man, I went out with him, but as soon as things got intimate I wasn't able, I couldn't let anyone else touch me, it made me feel bad. I understood that in that case I wouldn't be cheating on him, but I would be cheating on myself.

I was very ill, I didn't sleep, I didn't eat, I had become anorexic, I literally lacked physical strength, I struggled to cope with some social commitments, after which I immediately went to lie down on the bed, locked in my room. I cried and reproached myself for every mistake I may have made, every wrong word, every gesture I should or should not have made. My husband hadn't even noticed my depression and anorexia, he hadn't seen me around the house weighing 40 kilograms, I who am 1.75 meters tall, he didn't notice anything strange, my tiredness and my apathy only annoyed him.

On the advice of a friend, I went to talk to a lawyer about a possible divorce. The thought alone terrified me.

The lawyer received me in his luxurious office and, after examining my situation, he told me full of himself: 'We will make him pay dearly. He will pay, he will pay, he will pay.' He taught me how to spy on my husband, how to provide data on his business and his private life...

Chapter 5

From the stars
to the stables

I went home feeling dirty, filthy and tired. I decided not to follow the lawyer's advice.

I continued to feel bad. I went to see a psychiatrist. Of course, the psychiatrist prescribed me several psychotropic drugs that I had to take in the morning, at lunch and in the evening. Every day of my life. Something inside me was still reasoning, telling me: Giuliana, you are not on the right path. But I still did not know what to do.

I spent another period of inertia in my depression.

One day, a friend visited me and took me to a boutique where they sold small animals. It was there that I saw a small white dog and, once I picked him up, he became part of my life, my companion and my care. He started making me smile, I went out running with him and I started eating and smiling again. My situation hadn't changed, but my state of mind was changing, I was starting to contemplate life again and I wasn't thinking about suicide anymore. The problems were the same, but now I was smiling and moving again thanks to my little friend.

Little by little I got back on my feet, I don't know what motivation I had found inside me but, one day, I remember it was a warm Sunday in spring, I put the dog in the car, some clothes, my documents, some savings I had, I went to my husband and I said: 'I'm leaving now'. He didn't ask me not to go, not even where I was going, where I would be, what I would do, he simply replied 'Okay'.

I got into the car and drove down the driveway that led to the exit of the property, and before turning, before the image of the beautiful villa, the garden, the pool, and my husband, there, on the driveway, faded, I turned around for the last time. He was no longer there, not a hello, not a hug, no 'I'll call you', no 'if you need me call me', nothing..... no one wanted me back, no one cared. My car crossed the gate of the property, and so, one Sunday in spring, I, Giuliana Misir, found myself on the road, in my car, with my dog, and I didn't know where I would go and what I would do.

Get up and walk!
(Gospel according to John)

I would like to know, my dear friend, what your thoughts are on the story I just told, a personal story, sadly carried on for 10 years of my life.

I've kept it short, leaving out the ugly details—the arguments, the sleepless nights, and all the misery that comes when two people no longer love each other, or, worse, when a relationship ends because your partner no longer loves you.

When your partner no longer loves you and you, instead, love him, this is the wound that disables you, makes you feel like you are worthless, you are not good enough for him, you are probably not good enough for anyone in the world.

Dear friend reading these lines, if this has never happened to you, lucky you, blessed you, carry this light forward with you, the light of loving and being loved. Expand this love you feel to everyone else in the world and your aura will increase, your energy will increase, your personality will be able to expand and so, being joyfully open to life, because love gives you this strength, you will open new doors, you will climb higher in your evolution and everything will be better and better. Remember to maintain and nurture this state of love for yourself, your partner, your family, spread it to the world and the world will reciprocate by always giving you something beautiful.

But at that moment this wasn't my situation and it probably isn't the situation of many women in the world now.

The trauma of a broken bond, a lack of love, or the wounds received during a toxic relationship are, for the soul, comparable to a debilitating physical illness. If this state of trauma and suffering persists, the illness will also manifest itself physically, since, as we all know, the soul and body are connected.

I immediately focused on work, to shift the focus from personal problems to a new life, for the moment only work, but which absorbed my thoughts and energy throughout the day in another direction, even if returning home in the evening was sometimes difficult. I was lucky to have my little dog who continued to be my baby, my playmate and the cure for my anxieties.

Get up and walk!
(Gospel according to John)

Initially, I struggled to maintain the image of an independent and self-sufficient woman, but over time, through working, I truly became independent and self-sufficient. Then, over the years, I was able to return to the standard of living I had previously lived.

I haven't stopped thinking about my physical appearance; I've done yoga, Pilates, and swimming. Exercise also helps you psychologically. Walking in the beautiful nature has also been a cure. Cry if you feel like it, but then dry your eyes and get out of the house. Go exercise, play sports, read, find a job that demands the most from you. It's a great way to grow.

How do you get up after a deep crisis, after a trauma, after a failure?

There are no one-size-fits-all rules; everyone must find their own way and path. But, again, to get started, I'd recommend reviewing the basic rules listed at the beginning of the book. That's the first step, then everything else will follow. Never, ever wait for the universe to send you the big lottery win while you sit at home watching Netflix. Wins and rematches will come if you have discipline and method with yourself, if you don't give up even after multiple failures, because remember, you will control the world when you control yourself.

The Billion Dollar Superwoman Mindset

*E*ven if you currently have little money and many dreams, if you're reading this book, you're definitely becoming that billion-dollar superwoman. A desire to fully develop your personality on all levels is growing in your soul, and your mind is trying to find a method or means to achieve it. And...the mind creates! What you see in your mind will happen in reality. Imagine! You can! The more you dream of what you want to become, the more you will become it. Allow yourself to dream of what you want to be and how you want to become as many times as you want, because what you create in your mind will sooner or later materialize in your real world, in your life. And....the mind creates! What you see in your mind will happen in reality. Imagine! You can! The more you dream of what you want to become, you will become it. Allow yourself to dream of what you want to be and how you want to become as many times as you want, because what you create in your mind will sooner or later materialize in your real world, in your life.

The billion-dollar superwoman isn't always financially wealthy (though she often is or becomes so), but that's her potential, a potential of the highest order. She's elevated in every sense and creates a positive, superior atmosphere around her, thus attracting like-minded people, men or women. That's why very often, almost always, such a woman marries a billionaire. It can't be otherwise.

1. Superwoman always has a positive thought towards everything she does.

2. Superwoman is never afraid.

3. When superwoman thinks about doing something, she never contemplates the possibility of failure.

   Because she is organized, thinks positively, and is fearless, failure almost never happens.

   If that happens, she is able to try again and succeed.

4. Superwoman has self-confidence.

The Billion Dollar Superwoman Mindset

5. Superwoman is free from the past. She doesn't let past experiences dictate her; she lives in the here and now.

    Whatever happened in the past, the present experience of the here and now is completely new.

6. The superwoman has trained herself to think 'out of the box', she analyses the situation she finds herself in well, therefore she is difficult to manipulate.

7. The superwoman is gifted with a strong intuition (we all have it but we don't listen to it) that knows how to listen and evaluate.

8. A superwoman never repeats the same mistake. She knows it would lead to the same problem again... No.

9. Superwoman knows how to avoid people below her spiritual and energetic level; they would bring her down to their level. In Italy, there's a saying: "Better alone than in bad company."

10. The superwoman knows how to love on a higher level, but she also knows how to withdraw at the right time from a relationship that may be toxic.

    Many men say: 'I've had many women, but she has remained in my heart.'
    That was the superwoman who walked through his life.

11. Superwoman always strives higher; her limit is the sky.

12. Superwoman knows how to be alone.

    The superwoman doesn't need anyone around her, she is complete, she is the master of her thoughts, her actions, her life plans.

    If she chooses to be with someone, it's not to feel complete (because she already is), but to give and receive love, which is the true meaning of life.

The Billion Dollar Superwoman Mindset

13. Superwoman needs more personal space than average. I'm referring not just to physical space, but also to energetic, vital space. Her person is like an entire planet, not a satellite orbiting someone.

14. The superwoman chooses to be with a superman. With a partner who isn't on the same level, the relationship won't work, but she will leave an indelible mark on her partner's life, one that will forever be remembered.

15. Because she is much better than average, the superwoman will have fewer friends but deeper and more authentic bonds.

16. The superwoman knows how to be a wonderful wife (in every sense of the word), a true resource for her husband and a supermom for her lucky children to whom she will pass on her sense of stability and security.

17. When she completes her evolution, a superwoman is a person who can easily achieve success in whatever she wants.

Chapter 8

*H*ere are the signs that you are becoming or already are a superwoman

1. You will gain more confidence and self-assurance, so your new strong and confident personality may be interpreted by many as arrogant.

Weak people instinctively fear strong and confident people. They call it arrogance when someone in a certain way stands out from the crowd, doesn't fit the 'standards' of the average individual.

That's why not everyone will like you. Don't worry, it's natural selection. Over time, you'll have other people like you around you.

2. There is also the category, let's say, of the average man, the poor one who doesn't stand out from the crowd, the one who in life only knows how to cheer for his team, have a mediocre job and do nothing important in life. Know that this type of man is frightened by an evolved superwoman, with a high level of creativity and energy, often with a beautiful appearance. Well, yes. Know that this entire category of men is frightened by you. You make them uncomfortable. They will want to be with their female counterpart. They won't like you. Thank goodness.

3. You'll sometimes feel the envy of others. If they envy you, it's a sign you're on the right track.

Stay well away from envious people; they will only slow down your evolution.

4. You'll attract friends like you. You'll have a great bond with them. Hurray!

5. You will attract men like you, beautiful, evolved, confident men with strong personalities, high energy levels, and an excellent capacity for love.

An evolved and complete Superman desires nothing more than to have a superwoman with him who empowers him and nourishes his masculine energy, while he will increase your feminine energy.

Chapter 8

Within such a union, you will be able to express your immense potential by giving strength to your partner. You will be like a tree in bloom. Bloom, baby, bloom.

There's also a bonus: very often, the evolved Superman you meet is also, indeed, a special person, above average, with a lot of energy and creativity. Often, he has already achieved financial wealth (or is well on his way to it).

The billion-dollar superwoman is naturally made for a multi-billion-dollar superman. Bang!

6. Over time, you'll realize that wealth is also love—a lot of love, a passion for the things you do (which will then bring you money), incredible energy and a zest for life, a constant curiosity about the universe around you, and a joy for living.

Chapter 9

This is not goodbye

My dear friend, if you have read this short guide, it means that your transformation has already begun.

I can only be happy for you, and if this little book of mine can help you, I thank you, because I'm happy to help.

You'll probably have other inspiration and help in life too, because when you look for something, you'll find it, I can assure you.

Use your mind to make plans and programs, dream your dreams will come true.

Sure, put in the work to get what you want, work on yourself, and on things. Everything you want will come true.

If you want my advice, don't talk about your plans, just put them into practice. Your success will speak volumes.

Remember to love yourself and give love.

If you happen to be alone, know that loneliness is not a problem, but a wonderful opportunity to take care of yourself. When you reach a certain level of energy and personality, the right person for you will come along. You don't have to search. You just have to BE. Everything else will come to you.

Always take deep breaths, try to go into nature, eat healthily and in small amounts, and fast sometimes if you can.

Have sex, even with yourself.

Keep your beautiful body moving.

Laugh and cry whenever you feel the need.

Dress smart and be smart.

Chapter 9

This is not goodbye

Nourish your soul with beauty; remember that's what art, literature, history, and travel are for. Seek out all that is beautiful, because our soul is a mirror; we display what we've contemplated, what we've nourished.

If you think it might be useful, please pass this guide on to a friend who you think needs it.

If you've read this little guide of mine up to this point and have decided to follow our philosophy of female life, I know you're becoming a billion-dollar superwoman.

A hug from my heart to your heart,

With love,

Giuliana Misir